GOING BEYOND
GRATITUDE

Rewire Your Brain, Develop a Gratitude Mindset, Find Peace Within, and Start Your Day With Positivity

By

SANYA KAPOOR

ACKNOWLEDGMENT

I am immensely thankful to the Universe for aligning everything in my life so perfectly. Every step, every challenge, and every triumph has been part of a grand design to bring me closer to my true purpose. The Universe, in its infinite wisdom, has been my silent partner, always guiding me toward what I wanted, and more importantly, what I needed to evolve.

My deepest gratitude goes to my parents, the ones who brought me into this beautiful world. You both have been my constant source of energy and strength. When no one else believed in me, you did. You pushed me to become the best version of myself, always striving for growth. Your unwavering belief in me is the foundation of my success, and for that, I am eternally grateful.

To my mentors, Mitesh and Indu Khatri, I dedicate this book and the "Sanya 2.0" version of myself to you. You have been my guiding force, showing me the way when I needed it most. Words cannot capture the depth of my love and appreciation for both of you.

A special thank you to my life partner, Sajal. You have stood by me, not just in tough times but in every moment, helping me find my way to becoming a life coach. Your unwavering support and the stability you bring to my life are gifts from the Universe. I feel blessed beyond measure to have you by my side, especially as I write my first book. Your belief in me is beyond words.

To my siblings, Vansh and Manya, thank you for reminding me that I am capable of doing far greater things. Your encouragement has been a light in my journey, and I am grateful for your presence in my life.

To those who helped me so generously during the pre-launch of this book—Vanshika Goyal, Prem Kedia, Sajal Khanna, Rishi Jha, Vinay Keshri, Yashaswini Sharma, Kartikay Singhal, Rakshit Mehrotra, Ashish Pathak, Siddharth Mitra, and Khushboo Kapoor—thank you for showing up with your love, energy, and support. Each of you has played a role in making this dream come true, and I'm deeply grateful.

Finally, to all my readers, I dedicate this book to you. Thank you for being part of my journey. Each one of you is special, and I am filled with immense gratitude for your presence in my life. Together, we walk this path of growth, love, and gratitude.

Why Is This Book For You?

Thank you for choosing this book and for being a part of my journey. I believe the practice of gratitude has the power to transform lives, and it is my hope that this book helps you unlock that magic in your own life.

As you turn each page, know that you are embarking on a journey of self-discovery, love, and abundance. Gratitude has been the guiding force in my life, and I am honored to share the wisdom and practices that have enriched my world with you.

This book is more than words it's an invitation to shift your perspective, embrace the beauty around you, and cultivate a mindset that attracts more joy and fulfillment. I'm deeply grateful for your support and trust in allowing me to be part of your growth.

Remember, as you read and practice the ideas in these pages, you are capable of achieving incredible things. Let gratitude be your guide, and watch as your life blossoms in ways you never thought possible.

When I first started my journey as a life coach, the one thing that profoundly changed my life was the daily practice of gratitude. If I can recommend one practice that you should do every single day, it's this: embrace gratitude. Trust me, by incorporating what you're about to learn, you will fall in love with life in a way you never thought possible.

Before we begin, let's take a moment to say thank you—to the Universe, to God, or to whatever higher power you believe in—for leading you to this moment. Remember, the gift of gratitude comes to you only through the will of the Universe. Let's express our thanks for that blessing, and then dive into the magic this book has to offer.

With love and gratitude,

Sanya Kapoor

Table Of Contents

CHAPTER 1

THE POWER OF GRATITUDE: UNLOCKING THE UNIVERSAL LAW

What is Gratitude?

"Gratitude is not only the greatest of virtues, but the parent of all others."

- Cicero

hy is Gratitude Important?

Before I tell you what gratitude is, let's talk about why it's so important. Many of us go through our daily lives without really noticing all the amazing gifts we already have. We're born into this world with so much to be thankful for, but sometimes it's just too easy to focus on what we don't have. When we do this, we end up complaining about little things, which can make life feel heavy and tough.

Think about it: when we complain, we start to lose sight of all the good stuff around us. This doesn't just make us feel down; it can also affect our health and our relationships. Constantly being negative can drain our energy, leaving us feeling unhappy and stressed. It might even make it harder for us to do well at work or connect with our friends and family.

Let me give you an example. Imagine you give a thoughtful gift to a friend. Instead of saying thank you, they complain that it's not what they wanted or that it could have been better. How would that make you feel? Pretty disappointed, right? You might think twice before giving them another gift in the future.

Now, let's switch it up. What if you gave a small gift to someone, and they genuinely loved it? They might say how much they appreciate it and how thoughtful you are. Doesn't that feel wonderful? When someone values your gesture, it makes you want to give even more!

This is exactly how the law of gratitude works! When we show appreciation for what we already have, we send a message to the Universe that we're open and ready for more good things. It's like saying, "Thank you for this! I'm excited to see what else is coming my way." The more we practice gratitude, the more positive experiences and opportunities seem to come our way.

When we change our focus from what we lack to what we already possess, it can really change our lives. Taking a moment to appreciate the little things—like a warm cup of coffee in the morning, a friendly smile from a stranger, or a cozy moment with our loved ones—can create space for happiness to fill our lives.

In a world that often highlights the negative, embracing gratitude can help us and those around us feel lighter and happier. It's like spreading sunshine! When we recognize and appreciate the good in our lives, we not only lift ourselves up but also inspire others to do the same.

You know, it's interesting how people often notice when someone's energy shifts. *I remember when my friend approached me one day and said, "What is it about you? You always look so happy and full of life. What's your secret?"*

At first, I was taken aback. I hadn't really thought about it. But then I realized it was all about gratitude. Ever since I started practicing it daily, I noticed a huge difference in my outlook. People would come up to me more often, saying there was something different about my energy. It was like I was radiating positivity.

Have you ever been around saints, gurus, or even just visited a temple? The atmosphere is incredible, right? That's the power of positivity, and it's something you can cultivate in your own life. When you focus on what you're grateful for—big or small—you start to see the world in a completely different light.

Practicing gratitude has transformed my perspective by 360 degrees. It's like a magical practice that helps you lift yourself up and, in turn, inspires others to feel lighter too. So, when I look around, I'm not just seeing challenges; I'm seeing opportunities for joy and appreciation. And that, I believe, is what makes the difference.

You know, it's puzzling that we're never really taught about gratitude in childhood. Just think—if we had learned about its power early on, our lives might look so different today! But I truly believe that discovering gratitude is something the universe reveals to us when the time is right. And since you're reading this, I feel like you've been chosen by those universal powers to transform your life.

Gratitude isn't a new concept; it's been celebrated across various cultures and religions for centuries.

For instance, in Hinduism, the Bhagavad Gita teaches us through Lord Krishna that performing our duties with gratitude brings purpose and fulfillment. In chapter 2, verse 47, it says, "You have the right to perform your prescribed duties, but you are not entitled to the fruits of your actions." This reminds us that when we focus on our responsibilities and appreciate the opportunity to contribute, we can find peace without being attached to the outcomes.

Similarly, in Christianity, there's a powerful reminder in 1 Thessalonians 5:18: "Give thanks in all circumstances; for this is the will of God in Christ Jesus for you." This verse encourages us to maintain a thankful heart, regardless of our situation.

Buddhism also emphasizes gratitude, highlighting that recognizing the kindness of others can lead to greater happiness.

In the Dhammapada, it says, "Let us rise up and be thankful," reminding us to cherish the small joys in our lives.

In Sikhism, the concept of Chardi Kala promotes a spirit of eternal optimism. The Guru Granth Sahib teaches that a grateful heart leads to a joyful life, encouraging us to appreciate the blessings we receive.

Lastly, the Qur'an beautifully expresses this idea in Surah Ibrahim 14:7: "If you give thanks, I will give you more of My Blessings." This verse highlights the reciprocal nature of gratitude— acknowledging our gifts opens the door to even more positivity in our lives.

So, gratitude isn't just a nice idea; it's a profound practice that many cultures have recognized for its transformative power. Embracing it can truly change how we experience the world!

So, before we dive into what gratitude really means, let's remember how powerful it can be in transforming our lives. Embracing gratitude is the first step toward opening the door to a world filled with abundance and joy.

****

The Magic of Gratitude

Hey there! I want to share something really special with you today: gratitude. You might have heard the word before, but let me tell you how magical it can be.

Gratitude is all about being thankful for what you already have. It's about noticing the good things in your life, no matter how small they are. It could be a warm cup of coffee in the morning, a smile from a friend, or even the beauty of nature around you.

When you take a moment to appreciate these little things, you begin to feel a shift in your heart.

You know what's amazing? Gratitude isn't just about saying "thank you." It's about really feeling that thankfulness. When you genuinely appreciate what's in your life, everything starts to change. Suddenly, things feel lighter, and you might even find that you're smiling more often.

"Gratitude turns what we have into enough."

Let me share a little story from my life. *There was a time when I had achieved many things I had worked hard for, but I still felt unhappy. I didn't understand why.*

One day, while I was deep in thought, I had a heart-to-heart talk with the Universe. That's when I discovered the power of gratitude.

When I started practicing gratitude, it was like a light bulb went off in my head! I began to feel happier and more at peace. People around me noticed, too. They told me I was glowing! This change came from within me, and it felt so good.

"Gratitude helps you fall in love with the life you already have."

One of the most magical things that happened when I embraced gratitude was attracting my life partner. For years, I was searching for the right person. I tried everything—dating apps, meeting people, you name it. But nothing seemed to work.

Then, I decided to change my focus. Instead of worrying about what I didn't have, I started feeling grateful for everything that was already in my life. That's when the magic happened.

I met my partner in my hometown, a place where we had both lived for years but never crossed paths. It's a small town, so it felt strange we hadn't met before.

I really believe the Universe waited for me to change my mindset—from one of lack to one of gratitude. Once I did that, the person I had been searching for appeared! Now, we share such a beautiful connection, and I'm so thankful for him every day.

Gratitude really does open doors you didn't even know existed. When you focus on the good, more good things come into your life. The more you practice gratitude, the more beauty you'll see all around you.

"Gratitude makes sense of our past, brings peace for today, and creates a vision for tomorrow." — Melody Beattie

So, how do you start practicing gratitude? It's super simple! Each day, take a moment—just a few minutes—to think about one or two things you're grateful for. They don't have to be big things. Maybe it's a delicious meal you had or a lovely chat with a friend. The important part is to feel that appreciation.

As you keep practicing gratitude, you'll notice your outlook on life starting to shift. You'll find more reasons to smile, and life will feel more joyful and peaceful.

Gratitude doesn't just change how you feel—it changes what you attract into your life. When you focus on the good, life gives you even more good things to appreciate.

Let's promise to live our lives with love, joy, and gratitude. We only get one chance at this life, so let's make it special! I know you'll start to see amazing changes, just like I did.

In the next chapters, I'll share easy ways to make gratitude a part of your daily routine. But for now, remember that gratitude is a gift you can give yourself every day.

You just need to choose to notice the good things! I hope you're excited to find out how this works! Together, we'll explore more about gratitude and learn how it can bring abundance into your life.

<u>Key Takeaways</u>

Understanding Gratitude: Gratitude goes beyond saying "thank you"; it's about genuinely appreciating what we have, fostering a positive mindset.

Shift in Focus: Focusing on what we already possess rather than what we lack can lead to significant personal transformation and improved well-being.

Impact on Health and Relationships: Practicing gratitude enhances our health and strengthens relationships by reducing negativity and fostering positivity.

The Law of Gratitude: Showing appreciation signals to the Universe that we are open to receiving more good things in life.

Daily Practice: Taking a moment each day to acknowledge one or two things we're grateful for can lead to a positive shift in perspective.

CHAPTER 2

SCIENCE BEHIND GRATITUDE

"Gratitude is the fairest blossom which springs from the soul."

- Henry Ward Beecher

<u>The Law of Attraction</u>

Gratitude is more than just a nice sentiment; it's a powerful force that shapes our experiences. According to the Law of Attraction, everything in the universe is energy. You are energy. I am energy. Even this book is energy. Our thoughts and feelings are also forms of energy, meaning that what we think and feel can attract similar experiences into our lives.

If we constantly dwell on negative thoughts feeling unhappy or believing that no one understands us we tend to attract more negative experiences. On the other hand, when we focus on positive thoughts, like appreciating our supportive friends or feeling grateful for our family, we send out positive energy that draws more good things our way.

Have you ever noticed that when you repeatedly tell yourself, "I don't want to be late today," you often end up being late? This happens because the energy created by that thought can lead to a series of events that culminate in exactly what you wanted to avoid. In a universe where everything is energy, our thoughts can manifest into experiences that align with them.

Let me share the story of my student, Harsh, who was preparing for his Articleship for the CA Final. He was really worried about getting an Articleship in the right place, and his constant anxious thoughts were holding him back. Harsh often thought things like, "What if I don't find a good firm?" or "I'm not good enough to get the Articleship I want." These worries created a negative energy that made him feel more stressed and uncertain.

During our 7-day program to transform his mindset, we focused on shifting his thoughts and cultivating gratitude. I encouraged Harsh to keep a daily gratitude journal, where he would write down three things he appreciated each day—whether it was support from friends, helpful study resources, or even his own efforts in preparing for his exams.

As he began to practice gratitude, he noticed a change in his mindset. Instead of fixating on his fears, he started thinking positively about his capabilities and the opportunities available to him. He realized he had skills to offer and began to focus on what he could bring to a firm rather than what he lacked.

By the end of the program, Harsh shared that he felt more confident and proactive. Instead of worrying about where he would end up, he began reaching out to firms and networking more. This shift in energy helped him attract better opportunities. Ultimately, he secured an Articleship at a firm that aligned with his goals and values.

Harsh's story illustrates how our thoughts can manifest into our experiences. By changing his focus from worry to gratitude and positivity, he not only eased his anxiety but also opened doors to the right opportunities.

<u>The Science of Gratitude</u>

Let's talk about gratitude and why it's so important. Giving gratitude is really about appreciating the good things in our lives. When we take a moment to say "thank you" or recognize what we're grateful for, it actually changes how we feel. It's like shining a light on the positives instead of letting the negatives take over our thoughts.

Imagine you're having a tough day and it feels like nothing is going right. If you pause and think about just one good thing—like a friend who called to check on you or a beautiful sunset you saw— it can lift your spirits. That small shift in focus helps you see that there is still goodness in your life, even when times are hard.

Let me share a story about my friend, Raj. He was going through a tough time and always focused on the negatives in his life, especially when it came to his family and his wife. Instead of seeing the good things she did, he often complained about little things. This was affecting his mood and their relationship.

I wanted to help him, so I suggested he start a gratitude journal. I encouraged him to write down three things he appreciated each day—about his wife or his life. At first, it was hard for him. But soon, he started noticing small things, like "She made my favorite breakfast" or "She smiled when I got home."

As he practiced gratitude, he began to feel happier and lighter. He realized how much his wife was doing for him, even if he hadn't noticed it before. This change in mindset made him more affectionate and caring. Their conversations became friendlier, and they started enjoying their time together again.

In just a few weeks, Raj transformed his outlook. By appreciating the small things, he not only felt better himself but also grew closer to his wife. It was amazing to see how a simple change in thinking could lead to such positive changes in his life

Gratitude isn't just about saying "thank you"; it's an important feeling that can make us happier and healthier. When we feel grateful, our brains release chemicals like dopamine and serotonin, which are known to make us feel good. Studies have shown that gratitude lights up parts of our brains related to rewards and friendships. So, being grateful not only lifts our mood but also helps us connect better with others.

Research shows that practicing gratitude can improve our mental health. People who keep gratitude journals or regularly express thanks often feel less depressed and anxious. Psychologists like Robert Emmons and Michael McCullough have found that focusing on what we're thankful for makes us more optimistic and satisfied with life. This shift helps us see the good things we have instead of worrying about what we lack.

Gratitude also positively impacts our physical health. Grateful people tend to take better care of themselves—they exercise more, sleep better, and are less likely to abuse substances. One study found that those who practice gratitude report fewer health problems and are more likely to visit the doctor when needed. This might be because feeling good helps strengthen our immune system.

Another great thing about gratitude is how it spreads. When we show gratitude, we not only feel better ourselves but also make others feel good. This creates a sense of community and support around us, benefiting everyone. Gratitude helps us build stronger connections and promotes positive feelings.

The best part is that gratitude is something we can practice and improve. Simple activities like writing in a gratitude journal, sending thank-you notes, or just taking a moment each day to think about what we appreciate can help us become more grateful. Even small, regular acts of gratitude can make a big difference in how we feel.

When you express gratitude, it creates positive energy. It's like sending out a signal to the universe that you appreciate what you have. The more you practice gratitude, the more good things seem to come your way. It's a cycle: the more you focus on gratitude, the more reasons you find to be grateful.

Research supports this idea. Studies show that people who regularly express gratitude experience increased happiness and reduced stress. One study published in *Psychological Science* found that individuals who keep a gratitude journal—writing down what they are thankful for—report higher levels of life satisfaction.

In short, gratitude can make us happier and healthier. By understanding how it works, we can bring more gratitude into our daily lives and attract more positivity.

When we embrace gratitude, we not only improve our own lives but also uplift those around us, creating a happier and more supportive world.

<u>Lessons from Spiritual Texts</u>

Spiritual texts from various traditions emphasize the importance of gratitude in our lives. In the Ramayana, Lord Ram exemplifies gratitude by honoring and valuing his mother, even in challenging circumstances. His actions serve as a reminder for us to appreciate those who support us, highlighting the importance of recognizing the love and help we receive from others.

Similarly, in the Bhagavad Gita, Lord Krishna encourages us to accept everything with joy. He teaches that performing our duties with a mindset of gratitude leads to inner peace. When we focus on what we have instead of what we lack, we uncover deeper happiness and fulfillment.

Simple Ways to Practice Gratitude Daily

Incorporating gratitude into your daily routine can be simple and rewarding. Here are a few easy ways to make gratitude a part of your life:

<u>Start a Gratitude Journal</u>: Each day, write down three things you're thankful for. They can be small, like enjoying a sunny day or sharing a laugh with a friend. This practice helps you notice the good in your life.

Express Gratitude to Others: Take a moment to tell someone how much they mean to you. A quick text or a kind word can brighten their day and strengthen your connection.

Notice the Little Things: Throughout your day, pay attention to small blessings that often go unnoticed—a gentle breeze, a delicious meal, or a kind smile from a stranger. These moments add up to a happier life.

Say "Thank You" Often: Make it a habit to express gratitude regularly, even for simple things. Saying "thank you" reinforces a mindset of appreciation and invites more positive experiences.

The Impact of Gratitude

As you practice gratitude more, you'll likely notice a shift in your outlook. Life will feel brighter, and you'll find more reasons to smile. Gratitude doesn't just change how you feel; it changes what you attract into your life. By focusing on the positive, you invite even more good things to come your way.

Think about it this way: if you tell someone how much you appreciate them, it strengthens your connection. They feel good, and it makes you feel good too! When you express gratitude, you're not just making someone else happy; you're also boosting your own happiness.

Embracing gratitude is a gift you can give yourself every day. While it may take some effort to recognize the good in your life, the benefits are incredible. Research has even shown that practicing gratitude can lead to improved mental and physical health. For instance, people who express gratitude are less likely to suffer from stress-related health issues and more likely to enjoy better sleep quality.

Conclusion

Practicing gratitude is a simple yet powerful way to change how you feel and what you attract into your life. It's all about noticing the little things and being thankful for them. By doing this regularly, you can create a more positive and fulfilling life.

Let's begin this journey of gratitude together, welcoming the beauty in our lives and inviting more positivity into our hearts. When we embrace gratitude, we open the door to a life filled with joy and abundance.

Here's a concise summary of the science behind the Law of Gratitude in bullet points:

Summary of the Science Behind the Law of Gratitude

- Energy and Attraction: Everything in the universe, including our thoughts and feelings, is energy. The Law of Attraction states that like attracts like, meaning our thoughts can draw similar experiences into our lives.

- Positive vs. Negative Focus: Focusing on negative thoughts (e.g., dissatisfaction with work) can attract more negative experiences. Conversely, concentrating on positive thoughts (e.g., appreciation for supportive friends) generates positive energy that attracts good things.

- Spiritual Lessons:

  o In the *Ramayana*, Lord Ram exemplifies gratitude by honoring his mother, highlighting the importance of appreciating those who support us.

  o In the *Bhagavad Gita*, Lord Krishna teaches us to accept everything with joy and perform our duties with gratitude, leading to greater inner peace.

- Impact on Emotions: Practicing gratitude shifts our emotional state, helping us to recognize the good in our lives. It acts as a counterbalance to negative feelings, lifting our spirits during tough times.

- Positive Energy Creation: Expressing gratitude generates positive energy, sending signals to the universe that we appreciate what we have. The more we practice gratitude, the more positive experiences we attract.

- Scientific Evidence: Research shows that gratitude enhances mental and physical health. Studies indicate that keeping a gratitude journal can increase life satisfaction, lower stress levels, and improve overall well-being.

- Daily Practices: Simple practices, such as maintaining a gratitude journal, expressing appreciation to others, and acknowledging small blessings, can incorporate gratitude into daily life, leading to long-term benefits.

- Strengthening Connections: Expressing gratitude not only boosts our happiness but also strengthens our relationships, fostering a sense of community and connection.

- Overall Life Improvement: Embracing gratitude creates a positive feedback loop, making it easier to notice and attract more good things into our lives.

Day 1 Assignment: Embrace the Power of Gratitude and Visualize Your Desires

Now that you've learned about the power of gratitude and how it influences your life, it's time to put it into practice. Let's begin by focusing on what you want to manifest in your life, followed by reflecting on gratitude.

Step 1: Write Down What You Want in Life

Take 10 minutes to write down, in detail, all the things you want to manifest in your life. Be as specific as possible. Whether it's a dream job, better health, deeper relationships, or a particular lifestyle—describe it clearly.

- Ask yourself:

  o What kind of life do I want to live?

  o What kind of people do I want around me?

  o What kind of work or personal success do I envision?

Step 2: Make a List of Things You Are Grateful For

Next, take 10 minutes to reflect on your current blessings:

1. Use the following format to express your gratitude:

  o "I am truly grateful for ___________ because ___________."

  o or "Thank you, Universe, for ___________ because ___________."

2. Include "because" in your statements to deepen your sense of gratitude.

3. Count Your Blessings: Reflect on simple blessings like having a home, access to food, clean water, and loving relationships.

Step 3: Connect with Gratitude

As you write down what you desire, feel grateful for these dreams as if they are already on their way to you. This sense of gratitude will boost the energy you're putting out into the universe, aligning you with the things you want.

CHAPTER 3

GRATITUDE AND CONNECTION - STRENGTHENING RELATIONSHIPS

"Gratitude is the glue that binds love together."

- Tony Robbins

The Transformative Power of Gratitude in Relationships

Have you ever found yourself wondering why we sometimes lose touch with friends or feel distant from family? Where does the tension start, and how does it grow?

Relationships are the heartbeat of our lives, and when they falter, everything else seems to follow. Imagine, for a moment, a world where you are the only person on earth. How would you feel if there was no one to share your happiness, sadness, or even a simple compliment? Loneliness would overwhelm you, right? It's in our relationships that we find our greatest joy and, at times, our deepest pain.

I learned this lesson the hard way in my late twenties. Back then, I had almost lost every meaningful relationship in my life. Overwhelmed with complaints and disappointments, I failed to see the simple truth: **the power of my words**, especially the complaints I voiced, even when they weren't directly to the people I was upset with. The energy of complaints, whether shared behind someone's back or out loud, has the power to erode the very foundation of relationships.

Complaints vs. Gratitude: The Hidden Forces in Relationships

It may sound surprising, but **complaints** are often at the root of relationship problems. Science backs this up. Studies show that homes where gratitude is practiced tend to be more peaceful, with closer, more connected relationships. Think about it: for every complaint, we should express **ten instances of gratitude** to truly nourish and maintain our bonds. Yet, how often do we do that?

How many times do we find ourselves focusing on what's wrong instead of what's right? This imbalance creates the chasm that separates us from the people we love.

Gratitude works like magic. It strengthens relationships, transforming how we view others and, in turn, how they respond to us. I witnessed this transformation firsthand through the experience of a friend, Megha. *She had been deeply frustrated with her partner, often focusing on the things that annoyed her. This focus on the negative began to take its toll, and her relationship began to crumble.*

But when Megha made a decision to practice gratitude—to consciously appreciate her partner for the little things he did, even something as small as his smile or his patience—everything began to shift. Over time, the tension dissolved, and their relationship flourished into something more loving than ever before. This simple practice of daily gratitude changed the entire dynamic between them.

How Gratitude Heals Relationships

When you start practicing gratitude, it's like shifting your energy. Instead of focusing on the flaws of others, you focus on their strengths. **The Law of Attraction** tells us that what we focus on grows. When you focus on negativity, it multiplies. But when you focus on the positive aspects of someone—whether it's a partner, a friend, or a colleague—the energy between you shifts, and the relationship blossoms.

Take the case of another friend of mine, Ruchi, who had been estranged from her sister for years. A series of misunderstandings had led to distance and silence between them. But Ruchi, determined to change the dynamic, began practicing gratitude. She started remembering the good times they had shared and appreciating the qualities she admired in her sister. Slowly but surely, their relationship healed. It wasn't long before they were laughing together again, their bond stronger than it had ever been.

The Law of Attraction and Relationships

Gratitude doesn't just change how we interact with others; it changes how we think. When we begin to feel grateful, we stop trying to change the other person. Instead, we accept and appreciate them as they are. This simple shift leads to deeper connections, more fulfilling relationships, and a stronger bond.

One of the most profound examples of how gratitude can transform relationships came from a woman I once worked with. She was in her late 50s, and her relationship with her husband had been troubled for decades. They barely spoke, and there seemed to be no love left between them. He had never even bought her flowers, and she felt neglected and unappreciated.

But when she decided to start practicing gratitude, everything changed. She stopped focusing on what was wrong with him or their marriage, and instead, she began to express appreciation for the small things he did. She thanked him for being there, for his quiet presence, for their shared history. Slowly, the dynamic shifted. One day, she told me, with tears in her eyes, that her husband had brought her flowers—something he had never done in their entire marriage. He even started taking her out on dates again, as if they were in their 20s. For the first time in years, they truly connected.

*Their relationship was transformed—not by forcing change, but by changing the energy between them. **Gratitude** had brought them back together.*

The Ripple Effect: How Gratitude Impacts Other Areas of Life

Not only does gratitude strengthen relationships, but think about it: the most common problems we face in life often stem from **relationship issues**. When our relationships are strained, it's difficult to focus on work, career, or money. Everything seems interconnected. Have you noticed that people with thriving businesses and abundant wealth also tend to have healthier relationships? That's not a coincidence. It's a result of harmony in multiple areas of life.

When you focus on one area to the exclusion of others—say, pouring all your energy into your career or your finances, while neglecting your personal relationships—you can't truly thrive. All four key areas of life—**health, relationships, wealth, and personal growth**—are connected. If you want to enjoy success in your career, you need to learn how to strengthen your relationships. You can't separate the two. **Give love and receive love** in every area of life, and everything will begin to flourish.

Life is beautiful, but it's only truly enjoyable when we **shift our energy** in the right direction. **Gratitude** is the key to unlocking that shift. The more we appreciate the people around us—just as they are—the more we open the door to love, joy, and fulfillment. When you start focusing on gratitude, every day becomes a gift. The months and years ahead will feel filled with love, growth, and abundance.

How Gratitude Transformed a Career

I once had a friend who had been stuck in a job for six years. She had been trying to get a promotion but had found no progress. Frustrated, she came to me for advice, and I suggested she focus on gratitude—

not just for the things in her life, but for her colleagues, her boss, and her work environment.

She was skeptical at first, but she decided to give it a try. She began focusing on what she appreciated about her workplace—her colleagues' hard work, her boss's support, and even the challenges that helped her grow. Within a few weeks of practicing gratitude daily, she started to notice changes. Her energy was different—more positive, more accepting—and people around her began to respond. She got a call for a promotion within the next month. Her career, which had been stagnant for years, began to take off, and she realized that her relationships at work were the key to unlocking new opportunities.

How to Practice Gratitude in Your Relationships

If you want to transform your relationships, I encourage you to start practicing gratitude today. Here's a simple exercise to get you started:

1. **Choose a Relationship**: Think of one person in your life with whom you'd like to see a positive shift. It could be a partner, family member, friend, or even a colleague.

2. **Express Gratitude for Their Qualities**: Look at a photo of this person (if available), and say "thank you" for at least five qualities you love about them. Focus on the things you

admire, whether it's their sense of humor, patience, or how they support you.

3. **Repeat Daily**: Do this exercise three times a day for a week. Notice how your perspective begins to shift. You'll start to feel more connected, and the relationship will naturally begin to improve.

Let me help you with some examples of how to express gratitude to different people in your life, depending on your relationship with them. These examples can give you inspiration for how to verbalize your appreciation in a way that feels authentic and meaningful.

****

Examples of Gratitude You Can Express

To Your Father:

- "I am truly grateful for my father for giving me the best education. Because of him, I have the skills and knowledge to pursue my dreams and enjoy the life I have today."

- "I am so thankful to my father for always being a pillar of strength and wisdom. His guidance has shaped me into the person I am today."

To Your Mother:

- "I am incredibly thankful for my mother's unconditional love and care. She has taught me the importance of compassion and kindness, which has guided me through every challenge in life."

- "I appreciate my mother's selflessness and dedication. She always puts others first, and I have learned so much from her example of love and resilience."

To Your Siblings:

- "I am grateful for my sibling's friendship and loyalty. We've shared so many wonderful memories together, and I know I can always count on them, no matter what."

- "I am thankful for the bond I share with my sibling. They've always been there to laugh with me, support me, and bring out the best in me."

To Your Friends:

- "I am incredibly thankful for my friends. They bring so much joy, laughter, and support into my life. I'm truly blessed to have such amazing people by my side."

- "I appreciate my friends for always being there when I need them, whether to celebrate my successes or help me through my struggles."

To Your Life Partner:

- "I am deeply grateful for my partner's love and companionship. Together, we build a life full of adventure, growth, and joy, and I cherish every moment we share."

- "I am truly thankful for my partner's unwavering support. They bring out the best in me, and our relationship strengthens me in ways I never imagined."

To Your In-Laws:

- "I am grateful for my in-laws for accepting me as part of the family. Their kindness and warmth have made me feel welcomed and loved."

- "I appreciate my in-laws for the wisdom they share. They have taught me so much about family, love, and tradition, and I am thankful for their guidance."

To Your Mentors:

- "I am incredibly grateful for my mentor's guidance and wisdom. Their advice has helped me navigate both personal and professional challenges, and I will always be thankful for their support."

- "I appreciate my mentor for believing in my potential when I couldn't see it myself. They've helped shape my path, and I will forever be grateful for their encouragement."

****

Assignment for Today: Practicing Gratitude in Your Relationships

Take 10 minutes today to try this exercise:

1. **Choose a Person**: Think of someone in your life who means a lot to you or someone with whom your relationship is currently strained.

2. **List 5 Things You're Grateful For**: Write down five specific qualities or actions of that person you are thankful for. It could be their smile, how they support you, or how they always make time for you.

3. **Say It Out Loud**: If possible, express this gratitude to the person directly. If not, simply reflect on it yourself, repeating your gratitude each day for a week.

Notice how this simple shift in focus transforms not only your relationship but also your overall sense of well-being. Gratitude is a powerful tool, and by using it, you'll find that your relationships become richer, deeper, and more fulfilling. Let's practice this together and experience the joy it brings!

Step 4: Optional Bonus

If it feels natural and safe, share your appreciation with them through a message or in person. Let it be heartfelt, not forced.

Reflection Prompts (End of 7 Days)

1. How has my perception of this person shifted?

2. Did I feel a difference in my own energy, mood, or thoughts?

3. Have I noticed any change in our interaction or connection?

4. What did this practice teach me about myself?

Chapter 4

Gratitude for Health

"A grateful heart is a healthy heart—gratitude lowers stress, boosts immunity, and brings the body into balance."

Thank you, universe, for making me realize the importance of health before it became too late. Health is a precious gift, yet many of us don't truly value it until we face health challenges. Are you someone who is grateful for your health every day, or do you only think about it when you're unwell?

On a scale of 1 to 10, how grateful are you for your health when you wake up in the morning or before you go to sleep? Many of us take our bodies for granted, assuming they'll function perfectly without much thought or care. But what if I told you that expressing gratitude for your health could improve it? In fact, gratitude is one of the fastest ways to enhance and enjoy your health fully.

Health is the greatest blessing given to us since birth. Our body is constantly working to keep us alive and well. If you start giving gratitude even a little bit for your health, you will begin to see small positive changes. And if you consistently express deep gratitude, you will start to see miracles in your health. Gratitude for one part of the body can also heal another part. If you're experiencing issues in one area, giving thanks for the health of other parts can lead to miraculous results.

My Own Journey of Healing Through Gratitude

Gratitude has completely changed how I treat my body. If you don't believe in the power of gratitude to heal, let me share my personal story. For years, I struggled with a nail fungus that caused intense pain. I consulted with top doctors and tried countless treatments, but nothing worked. In fact, my condition only worsened, and doctors told me that it couldn't be reversed. But I refused to accept that.

Instead of feeling defeated, I decided to practice gratitude. Each day, I thanked every part of my body, even my feet, visualizing them as healthy and beautiful. I imagined how my nails would look once healed and felt grateful for the future health of my feet. Just two years later, my nails are completely healthy and beautiful—without any medication. This is the power of gratitude. I feel immense gratitude for my body and the miracle it has experienced.

For a visual transformation, you can visit my YouTube channel to see the before and after pictures of my nails. Here's the link: UC6Ey-3KeBQW11OvNqWUnC0A

Research and the Power of Gratitude in Healing

Studies have shown that people who practice gratitude heal faster and are more likely to live longer—by as much as seven years! The law of attraction is simple: whatever you are grateful for, you attract more of. So, when you express gratitude for your health, you invite more health and vitality into your life. It's simple math.

When you begin to practice gratitude regularly, you'll notice improvements right away. Small discomforts, pains, or even scars can start to fade. You'll feel more energetic, positive, and connected to your body.

The Gift of Your Body: Inner and Outer Gifts

You know, your body is truly an incredible system—complex, resilient, and always working to keep you alive and thriving. Every part of it, from the top of your head to the tips of your toes, is designed with purpose, working tirelessly behind the scenes and in plain sight to support you in ways you might not even realize.

Let's take a moment to reflect together on the amazing gifts your body gives you—both the visible ones, the outer parts, and the unseen inner workings. By appreciating both, we can create a deeper connection with ourselves and the miracle of life that we experience every day.

Outer Body Parts: The Pillars of Movement and Expression

These are the parts that help you connect with the world around you—giving you the ability to move, interact, and express yourself. I want you to think about them for a moment, and really feel grateful for how they allow you to engage with everything around you.

- **Legs and Feet**: I want you to think about your legs and feet for a moment. They're the foundation that supports you through life. Whether you're walking, running, standing, or even just sitting—your legs and feet are there, holding you up. Every step you take is a blessing. Without them, imagine how different your experience of the world would be. Every time you move, every time you walk from one place to another, it's an opportunity to be grateful for these unsung heroes. Take a moment to thank your legs and feet for their endless support, for every step they've helped you take, and for the ability they give you to explore life.

- **Hands and Arms**: Now, let's think about your hands and arms. Your hands do so much for you—touching, creating, holding, expressing love, and connecting with the world. Have you ever paused to really think about all the little tasks your hands help you with every single day? Whether it's picking up a pen to write, typing on a keyboard, holding your phone, or hugging someone you care about—your hands are always working for you. Your arms give you the strength and reach to carry out all of these actions. Every time you create, work, or embrace someone, your arms and hands are your partners in doing so. Take a moment to express gratitude for them. Think of all the ways they've helped you engage with the world and the people in it.

- **Eyes**: Now, let's talk about your eyes. Without them, how different would life be? Your eyes are your windows to the world, allowing you to see all of the beauty and wonder that surrounds you. Every sunset, every face of someone you love, every detail you observe in nature—your eyes make it all possible. Take a second to think about how much you rely on your sight. Life would be so different without the ability to see, wouldn't it? So, right now, express gratitude to your eyes for giving you the gift of sight, for allowing you to experience life in vibrant colors, and for helping you connect with others through the expression in their faces.

- **Skin**: And your skin—let's not forget about this incredible organ. It's not just a protective barrier; it's what keeps you safe from the environment. It regulates your body temperature, shields you from harmful elements, and helps you sense the world around you. Without your skin, you'd be vulnerable to so many things. But it's more than just protection. Your skin lets you feel the touch of a loved one, the warmth of the sun, the coolness of a breeze. Take a moment right now to thank your skin for its role in keeping you safe and connected to everything around you.

****

Inner Body Parts: The Hidden Forces of Vitality

While you may not see them or think about them as much, your inner body parts work around the clock to keep you alive and functioning.

These inner organs and systems are constantly performing their duties without you even noticing. But their work is essential to everything you do.

- **Heart**: Think about your heart for a second. It's the heartbeat of your existence. It pumps blood, sending oxygen and nutrients throughout your entire body. Without your heart, you wouldn't be here. It's the center of life, the symbol of vitality. Just stop for a moment and feel the rhythm of your heart—steady, dependable, always working for you. Give thanks to your heart right now, for its unwavering work, for its tireless dedication to keeping you alive, and for its role in allowing you to love and experience life.

- **Lungs**: Every breath you take is a gift. Your lungs are responsible for bringing oxygen into your body and expelling carbon dioxide. Can you imagine what life would be like without the ability to breathe? With each breath, your lungs sustain you, filling you with life-giving oxygen. So take a moment now, inhale deeply, and express gratitude for your lungs. Thank them for the breath that fuels you every single moment, without fail.

- **Brain**: Your brain is where everything begins. It's the command center of your body, managing everything from your thoughts to your movements. Every decision you make, every memory you have, every new thing you learn—it all starts with your brain. Think about how much your brain does for you every day. It helps you think critically, problem-solve, express yourself, and even manage emotions. Take a moment to acknowledge the complexity of your brain and thank it for guiding you through life with intelligence, awareness, and insight.

- **Digestive System**: Now think about your digestive system, the unseen worker that processes everything you eat and drink. It breaks down your food, absorbs nutrients, and turns it all into energy that powers your body. It does this silently, without you ever needing to think about it. Yet, it plays a critical role in your health and well-being. Express gratitude for your digestive system, for the way it keeps you energized and nourished, allowing you to continue living fully every day.

- **Immune System**: Your immune system is always at work, protecting you from illnesses and infections you may never even know about. It's a silent, unseen defender, constantly on the lookout for any threat to your health. It keeps you strong, keeps you healthy, and shields you from harm. Take a moment to thank your immune system for its vigilance and its role in keeping you safe every day.

- **Kidneys and Liver**: Your kidneys and liver are responsible for filtering out toxins and waste from your body. They regulate your internal balance and keep everything functioning smoothly. These organs work tirelessly to ensure that you're healthy and balanced. So, pause for a moment and express gratitude to these incredible organs for their constant work behind the scenes, helping to detoxify your body and keep you feeling well.

****

Why Gratitude for Both Matters

When you take a moment to appreciate both your outer and inner body parts, you start to see just how miraculous your body really is. We often take our bodies for granted, don't we? We go about our day, unaware of all the incredible things happening inside and outside of us. But when you actively acknowledge the things you rely on—whether it's your hands that help you create, your lungs that fuel your breath, or your heart that beats for you—you develop a deeper connection with your body.

Gratitude not only makes you feel more alive, but it also strengthens your health. When you express thanks, you invite healing and positivity into each part of your body, and that energy ripples out to improve your well-being. When you acknowledge your body as a whole, you begin to recognize just how interconnected every part of you truly is.

****

The Real Cost of Neglecting Your Health

I want you to think about something for a moment. We often place value on things like money and possessions, but can you imagine how much each part of your body would cost if you had to buy it? Think about my own story with a simple nail fungus. It cost me ₹20,000 to treat it. That's just one small part of the body! Now, think about the value of your heart, your lungs, your legs. How much would all of those parts cost if you had to buy them?

The bare minimum cost for a simple disease treatment is ₹10,000. But that's just for a single treatment, and doesn't even take into account the emotional, physical, and mental toll it takes on you. We often don't realize how priceless our health is until something goes wrong. Imagine how much money we spend on medical bills that could have been avoided. Is that the kind of life you want to lead?

****

The Power of Gratitude and Words

Here's the beautiful thing: Gratitude is free, and it only takes 10 minutes of your day. Just 10 minutes of thankfulness for your body can make a world of difference. It brings joy, and a joyful mind creates a healthy body. There's so much science supporting this! Negative emotions, when stored in the body, can manifest as disease. I've seen this firsthand. My uncle used to be in constant pain—always angry, always complaining. His negativity took a toll on his health. But through positive thinking and gratitude, many of his issues began to heal.

The power of words is incredible. The things you say to yourself and about your health matter. Have you ever heard the phrase "Shubh Shubh Bolo" (speak positively)? It's not just an Indian tradition—it's rooted in science. When you focus on health, vitality, and positivity, you attract more of that into your life.

So today, start speaking positively about your health. Imagine a world where everyone spoke about their health with gratitude and love. That's a world full of thriving, happy people. And you can begin that change right now—starting with yourself.

Key Takeaways from Chapter 4: Gratitude for Health

- Health is a precious gift, but many of us only appreciate it when we face challenges. Practicing gratitude for your health can improve it and lead to positive changes.

- Regular gratitude for your body can enhance your health. Gratitude has the power to heal, even physical conditions, by thanking specific parts of your body.

- The author's experience with healing a nail fungus through gratitude demonstrates the effectiveness of this practice in improving health without medication.

- Research supports that gratitude can lead to faster healing, a longer life, and better overall health.

- When you consistently practice gratitude, you begin to notice improvements in your health—small pains fade, and energy levels rise.

- Outer body parts (legs, feet, hands, arms, eyes, skin) are essential for how we interact with the world. Regularly expressing gratitude for them strengthens your connection to your body.

- Inner organs (heart, lungs, brain, digestive system, immune system, kidneys, liver) work tirelessly behind the scenes to keep you healthy. Gratitude for these organs promotes overall well-being.

- Recognizing the interconnectedness of your body parts helps you see the holistic nature of health, where gratitude can nourish every part of you.

- Neglecting health can lead to hidden costs—financially and emotionally. For example, treating minor health issues like a nail fungus can cost a lot, highlighting how valuable good health truly is.

- Gratitude is a free, simple practice that can transform your life. Just 10 minutes a day of thankfulness can yield significant benefits for your health.

- Negative emotions can manifest as physical ailments. Practicing positive thinking and gratitude can counteract the negative impact of these emotions and promote healing.

- The words you use about your health matter. Speaking positively, like saying "Shubh Shubh Bolo" (speak positively), can attract more health and vitality into your life.

Assignment for Readers:

1. Gratitude Practice:

- **Objective:** Develop a daily gratitude practice to improve your health and well-being.

- **Instructions:**

  o For the next seven days, take 5–10 minutes each day to reflect on and express gratitude for different parts of your body.

o   Start with **outer body parts** like your legs, arms, hands, eyes, skin, and feet. Reflect on how they allow you to move, experience life, and connect with others.

o   Next, move to **inner body parts** like your heart, lungs, brain, digestive system, and immune system. Reflect on how they work behind the scenes to keep you alive and healthy.

o   You can either speak your gratitude aloud, write it down in a journal, or meditate on it.

o   At the end of the seven days, write down any physical or emotional changes you've noticed.

2. Health Reflection:

- **Objective:** Understand your relationship with your health and where gratitude can play a role.

- **Instructions:**

  o   Reflect on your current health status. On a scale from 1 to 10, how grateful are you for your health every day?

  o   Write about how you typically think of your health—do you take it for granted, or do you express gratitude for it regularly?

- List 3 specific things about your health that you are grateful for today. For example: "I am grateful for my heart that beats for me every second," or "I am thankful for my lungs that give me breath."

- Write about how practicing gratitude for your health could change the way you feel or the way your body functions.

3. Gratitude for Healing:

- **Objective:** Use gratitude to support healing or improvement in a specific area of your health.

- **Instructions:**

  - Choose a specific health issue or area of your body that may need healing (this could be a physical issue, emotional pain, or anything you feel needs attention).

  - Each day, spend 5 minutes focusing on this area and thank your body for its ability to heal and function.

  - Visualize healing in this part of your body, imagining it fully restored and healthy.

  - Write about any changes or shifts you experience in this area after a week of focusing on it with gratitude.

4. Financial Reflection on Health:

- **Objective:** Recognize the true cost of neglecting your health.

- **Instructions:**

  - Think about a time when you spent money on treating an illness, injury, or health condition. How much did it cost you in terms of money, time, and emotional well-being?

  - Reflect on how much your health is truly worth and how you can prioritize maintaining it through gratitude and self-care.

  - Write about how you can take better care of your health to avoid unnecessary medical costs in the future. How can you be proactive about your health every day?

5. Power of Words and Beliefs:

- **Objective:** Begin to shift your mindset by using positive language about your health.

- **Instructions:**

  - For the next 3 days, pay attention to the words you use when talking about your health. Do you often speak negatively or focus on what you don't want (e.g., "I don't want to get sick")?

o   Practice using positive language such as "I am healthy," "My body is strong," or "I am grateful for my vitality."

o   Write about how using positive language makes you feel. Do you notice any changes in your emotions or your physical state as a result of speaking positively?

6. Gratitude Journal:

- **Objective:** Develop a gratitude journal for health.

- **Instructions:**

  o   Start a daily gratitude journal dedicated to your health. Each day, write down at least 3 things you are grateful for regarding your body and health.

  o   Include both inner and outer body parts—things like "I am grateful for my heart that keeps me alive" or "I am thankful for my legs that carry me everywhere I go."

  o   At the end of the week, review your journal. How does it make you feel about your health? Has your perspective shifted over the week?

7. Future Vision:

- **Objective:** Visualize a healthy future.

- **Instructions:**

  - Take a few moments to close your eyes and imagine yourself in perfect health, physically, mentally, and emotionally.

  - Picture yourself living your best life—what are you doing? How does your body feel? What does your health allow you to experience in the future?

  - Write down this vision. What actions can you take today to make this vision a reality? How can gratitude help you maintain this state of health?

****

Reflection and Sharing:

- After completing these assignments, reflect on your journey with gratitude. How has your practice of gratitude affected your body, health, and mindset?

- Consider sharing your insights with someone else—perhaps a friend or family member—so you can encourage them to start their own gratitude practice for health.

Remember, gratitude is a simple yet powerful tool that can transform your relationship with your body and your health. Keep practicing and see how your life changes.

CHAPTER 5

THE POWER OF GRATITUDE FOR MONEY

"Gratitude turns what we have into enough, and opens the door to abundance."

Money, like every other thing in the universe, holds its own energy. When we fail to appreciate the money we have, we block the flow of abundance in our lives. If you're currently experiencing a lack of money, now is the perfect time to reflect on the energy and thoughts you direct toward it. Do you feel disappointment, nervousness, jealousy, or fear when you think about money? These emotions stem from a lack of gratitude, and they will only bring more scarcity into your life.

I remember one of my friends, Riya, who always felt anxious about money. She would constantly worry about her bills and compare herself to others, feeling as though she was stuck in a cycle of scarcity. However, once she shifted her mindset and started practicing gratitude for the small amounts she had, things changed. Riya stopped criticizing money and started thanking it, even for the smallest contributions. Over time, new opportunities for income opened up to her, and her financial situation improved drastically.

It's important to understand that like all things, the law of attraction works with money too. If you want to attract abundance, you must feel grateful for the money you already have. The famous saying goes, *"Whomsoever has gratitude will be given more, and they will have abundance. But whoever does not have gratitude, even what they have will be taken from them."* You might ask, "How can I feel grateful when I don't have abundance?" But this is precisely when gratitude becomes essential.

Practicing Gratitude for Past Money

Sit down in a peaceful place and reflect on all the ways money has supported you throughout your life. Were you always able to have food to eat? Water to drink? A home to live in? Think about your education—who paid for your school fees, lunches, and supplies? Even at birth, someone paid for your hospital bills. Birthdays, vacations, and moments of joy—were they funded by someone's money? You likely never felt a lack of money in childhood because the flow was there, even if it wasn't directly yours.

I had another friend, *Amit, who felt stuck financially for years. One day, he decided to sit down and list all the ways money had served him in his life—starting from childhood. From school supplies to family trips, he realized that money had always been present, even when he wasn't earning it. This practice helped him shift from a scarcity mindset to a state of gratitude, and soon after, new job opportunities came his way, and his finances improved.*

Gratitude for Present Money

Now, let's talk about the money you have right now. We all want more money, right? But have you ever taken a moment to feel genuinely grateful for what you have? Instead of focusing on the lack, or thinking, "How can I get more?" start appreciating what is already present in your life.

I used to make this same mistake. No matter how much I had, I always felt it wasn't enough. As a result, I kept attracting more bills and expenses. Why? Because my thoughts were focused on lack, not abundance. Once I shifted to gratitude, even for the little I had, things began to change. I attracted more money, and the bills became easier to handle.

When you're not grateful for your current situation—whether it's your home, your job, or your paycheck—you stop the flow of abundance. However, when you express gratitude for what you have, no matter how little, you open the door for more to come. Next time you pay a bill, do it with a grateful heart and bless the money you have. Say, "Wow, I'm so fortunate to have money to pay for this!"

Being Grateful for Money in Tough Times

I know it's hard to feel grateful when money is tight. But that's exactly when you need to practice gratitude the most. Gratitude is the secret to becoming a money magnet. When you're grateful, you raise your energy, and that energy attracts more wealth.

For instance, if you're paying rent, be grateful that you have a comfortable home to live in. Many people don't even have a roof over their heads. If you're paying for utilities like gas, water, or electricity, feel thankful for the comfort and convenience they bring into your life. If you're paying someone for their services, like a housekeeper, appreciate the time and energy they save you. Each of these small moments of gratitude will compound into larger feelings of abundance.

Beliefs About Money

Your beliefs shape your reality. If you believe that it's hard to make money, or that you'll never be wealthy because of your background, then that will be your reality. But if you can change your beliefs, you can change your financial future.

Limiting beliefs are like invisible barriers to success. I've heard people say, "I'll never be rich because I come from a poor family," or, "It's impossible to make money in this economy." These thoughts keep you stuck in the same cycle. But you can break free by changing your mindset.

The first step is to catch your negative self-talk. For example, if you often say, "I can't afford this," stop and replace that thought with, "I'm working toward being able to afford this." Repeating positive affirmations can transform your belief system and shift your energy toward abundance.

When you see something you desire—like a dream car or a beautiful home—start saying, "I can afford this." Even if it feels unrealistic at first, keep saying it until your belief changes. It worked for Amit. After changing his self-talk and adopting an abundance mindset, he was able to purchase the car he had always dreamed of.

Gratitude for Money and Abundance: A Simple Yet Powerful Shift

I want to share something truly transformative with you. A powerful practice that has the potential to shift your mindset and bring abundance into your life—something so simple, yet profoundly effective.

I know that many of us, when we go shopping, or when we see something luxurious—whether it's a beautiful car, a designer handbag, or even an extravagant home—our immediate thought often tends to be, "I can't afford that. It's out of my reach." I've been there too. I've felt that same sense of limitation and lack.

But what I'm about to share with you will change that completely, and it starts with something incredibly powerful—gratitude.

The Gratitude Practice for Abundance:

From today onwards, I want you to begin looking at every material thing you desire, every luxurious item, and every piece of abundance you see, not with feelings of longing or lack, but with a deep sense of gratitude. When you're in a store or you see a beautiful item or even when you pass a fancy car on the street, instead of thinking, "I can't afford that," pause and do the opposite—**feel grateful**.

Gratitude for the Money You Have Right Now:

You may not have everything you desire yet, but you have something very powerful right now—the money you currently have, and that in itself is worthy of gratitude. The very fact that you have the means to make purchases, to buy things, and to provide for yourself is something to be thankful for. Even if it's just enough for your daily needs, **be thankful for what you already have.**

You might say, "But I don't have enough for what I want," and that's okay. But here's the thing—gratitude is not about what you lack, it's about **what you already possess.** When you start feeling grateful for the money you have, you send a message to the universe that you **appreciate** and **value** what's already in your life. And that's when things begin to shift.

Transforming Your Mindset:

When you see something that feels beyond your current means, don't feel envy or lack. Instead, shift your perspective. **Say thank you.** Thank the universe for the money that is flowing into your life right now. **Say, "Thank you for this beautiful car. Thank you for the opportunity to experience such abundance. Thank you for all the financial opportunities that are coming my way."**

When you start feeling gratitude for something as simple as a car on the road or a luxurious item in a store, what you are actually doing is **aligning yourself with the energy of abundance.**

You're telling the universe that you recognize and appreciate abundance when you see it, and you are inviting it into your life.

The Universe's Subtle Messages:

Here's something truly amazing to consider: **Everything you see around you is the universe's way of showing you what is possible for you.** Every luxury item, every success story, every piece of wealth that catches your eye is simply a reflection of what's possible. It's not just something unattainable; it's the universe's way of telling you, "This can come into your life too." **This is a glimpse into your future.**

As you walk through your day, notice the abundance that surrounds you. If you see a beautiful house or a car that you desire, **don't feel lack**. Instead, feel an overwhelming sense of **gratitude**. Say to yourself, **"Thank you. Thank you for showing me what's possible. Thank you for this beautiful car, this beautiful home. I'm open and ready to receive this kind of abundance in my life."**

The Secret of Gratitude and Abundance:

Here's the magic: The more you practice gratitude for the abundance you see around you, the more **you will attract** that same abundance into your life. It's a law of the universe—what you focus on expands. When you focus on gratitude for the things you desire, when you appreciate the luxuries around you, you create a vibration that attracts more of that same energy.

It's like sending out a signal to the universe, saying, "I am ready for more of this." The universe responds to your energy and starts bringing more of those things into your experience.

So, every time you look at something you desire—whether it's a luxury bag, a new car, or a dream vacation—**feel thankful**. Let the gratitude flow from your heart and say, "Thank you for showing me what is possible. Thank you for bringing this into my life."

Remember, **gratitude is the magnet for abundance.** The more you practice it, the more the universe will align itself with your desires, bringing them to you in perfect timing.

****

Final Thought:

By practicing gratitude for the things you want, you not only shift your energy, but you also start to align your actions with that energy. You'll be amazed at how quickly opportunities start to appear, how your financial situation begins to improve, and how your entire outlook on life changes.

You are already on your way to attracting the abundance you deserve, and it all starts with a simple practice—being grateful for what you have now, and being thankful for the wealth that is on its way.

Start this practice today, and watch how your life begins to transform.

Transforming Jealousy into Gratitude: A Simple Yet Powerful Shift

Let me share something with you that can truly change how you look at the world—and more importantly, how you look at your own life and the things you desire.

I know, at times, it's easy to feel a sense of jealousy when we see someone else with something we really want. Maybe it's a beautiful home, a fancy car, a lifestyle that seems out of reach, or even a level of success we dream of achieving. You might catch yourself thinking, *"Why don't I have that?"* or *"That's so unfair. Why can't I afford that?"*

But let me tell you this: **Jealousy is a sign that you're on the wrong track.** It's a feeling that actually *pushes you away* from what you want.

When we feel jealous, we're focusing on lack. We're telling ourselves that what we want is out of reach. And in doing that, we're blocking ourselves from attracting those things into our lives.

Now, here's the powerful shift I want to offer you: **Instead of feeling jealous, choose gratitude.**

Next time you see someone with something you want, **don't think "I can't have that."** Instead, think of it as the universe giving you a *sign*. The fact that you're seeing someone with something you desire is actually a beautiful reminder that **it's possible for you too.**

Let me ask you this—there are **so many things in the world**. But why are you noticing **this particular thing**? Whether it's a car, a house, a piece of clothing, or a lifestyle—why is your attention drawn to it? **Because it's meant for you.** The universe is showing you something you can have too, if you open yourself up to it.

When you feel jealousy, it's like you're saying, "I can't have that." But instead, let's turn that energy around. **See it as a sign that you are capable of having exactly what you see.**

Here's how I want you to think about it:

The universe is showing you what's possible for your life. When you look at someone else's success or possessions, instead of feeling envious, stop and say to yourself, *"Thank you, God, for showing me that this is possible for me too."*

By doing this, you're recognizing that seeing it in someone else's life is actually proof that **it's on its way to you**. It's not out of reach. It's a reminder that abundance is flowing toward you.

So, from this moment on, whenever you feel jealous of something someone else has, I want you to stop and replace that feeling with gratitude. Be thankful, because the universe is showing you that this could be in your life as well. This isn't just some random coincidence—it's a sign that you're aligned with the energy of receiving it.

Here's how you can practice this:

1. **When you feel that twinge of jealousy, take a deep breath.**

2. **Shift your mindset:** Instead of thinking, *"Why don't I have that?"* think, *"Thank you for showing me that this is possible for me too. Thank you for this reminder that I can have this in my life."*

3. **Feel the gratitude rise inside you.** When you do this, you're telling the universe that you are ready and open to receive what you desire.

4. Watch how quickly your energy shifts. **You'll feel lighter, more positive, and you'll begin to attract more of what**

you want into your life, just by changing how you think about it.

The reality is, **jealousy will never bring you closer to your goals**. It will only make you feel like what you want is unreachable. But gratitude? Gratitude will *magnetize* what you desire and draw it closer to you.

****

Why Does This Work?

Because, when you practice gratitude instead of jealousy, you are aligning yourself with abundance. You stop focusing on lack, and instead, you focus on the **possibility**. You're essentially saying, *"I know this is available to me too. Thank you for showing me what is possible in my life."*

And that small shift in thinking is all it takes. When you feel thankful for what others have, instead of resenting it, you open yourself up to receive the same—and even more.

****

Let's Make This Shift Together:

- Next time you feel jealousy creeping in, stop, take a breath, and change the thought.

- Say: *"Thank you for showing me what is possible. I'm ready for this too."*

- Feel the gratitude for the sign the universe is giving you.

And let me tell you something—you'll be amazed at how quickly things start to shift. Gratitude will start bringing more opportunities, more abundance, and more of what you want into your life. When you shift from jealousy to gratitude, **you start to attract the very things you desire.**

****

I hope this message resonates with you, and I want you to remember this the next time you catch yourself feeling envious or jealous. **Gratitude, not jealousy, is the key to unlocking everything you want.** And it all starts with a simple mindset shift.

Thank you for being open to this, and I know that with this practice, abundance will start flowing your way.

Additional Tips to Amplify the Flow of Money

I want to share a powerful practice with you—something that can transform the way you experience money and bring more abundance into your life. Starting today, I encourage you to actively increase the flow of money by shifting your energy around it.

Here's the first part: **Do something generous**. Find at least five people today, whether they're friends, family, or even strangers, and offer them a helping hand. It doesn't have to be a large amount—what matters is the energy you're giving. You see, money is not just paper or numbers; it's energy. When you give with love, you're creating a positive flow of energy that comes back to you multiplied.

When you help someone out, you're not only uplifting them, but you're also inviting more abundance into your own life. This simple act of giving triggers a cycle of generosity that starts to expand your prosperity.

The second part of this practice is all about the energy of spending. Next time you pay for something—whether it's a bill, groceries, or even a cup of coffee—**say to yourself, "Go with love, grow with love."** Every time you exchange money, do so with gratitude and a mindset of abundance. Acknowledge that the money you're spending is helping to circulate the energy of prosperity in the world.

Feel thankful that you have the means to make the payment and to contribute to the flow of abundance in your life. The more love and gratitude you put behind your spending, the more you will attract opportunities to receive.

Remember: **money is a flow, not a finite resource**. By sending it out with love and appreciation, you signal to the universe that you're open and ready to receive even more.

Conclusion: The Law of Abundance

Remember, the universe responds to your energy. If you focus on lack, you'll attract more lack. But if you focus on abundance and practice gratitude, you'll attract more wealth into your life. Changing your mindset is simple but powerful. When you truly believe that you deserve abundance, the money will follow.

Start today. Be grateful for every cent, every opportunity, and every gift money has brought into your life. It's not about the amount—it's about the attitude. And once you cultivate gratitude, abundance will come naturally.

****

This chapter incorporates examples of how my friends Riya and Amit transformed their financial lives by practicing gratitude and changing their limiting beliefs.

Their stories are proof that with the right mindset, anyone can attract financial abundance.

Step 1: Reflect on Past Money

- List 5 moments where money supported you in the past (e.g., education, gifts, vacations).

- For each, say or write: *"I am grateful for the financial support I received."*

Step 2: Be Grateful for Present Money

- List 3 ways money is currently supporting you (e.g., paying bills, buying essentials).

- For each, say: *"Thank you, money, for helping me with [specific item]."*

- When paying a bill, say: *"I am grateful for the money to pay this."*

Step 3: Identify and Reverse Limiting Beliefs

- Write down 3 negative beliefs about money (e.g., "I can't afford this").

- Replace each with a positive affirmation (e.g., "I am attracting wealth").

Step 4: Practice Daily Abundance

- When you see something you desire, say: *"I can afford this."*

- At the end of the day, write down any moments of abundance (money saved, earned, or received).

Key Takeaways: The Power of Gratitude for Money

- **Money is Energy**: Treating money with appreciation helps attract more of it into your life.

- **Negative Emotions Block Abundance**: Fear, anxiety, jealousy, and scarcity-thinking around money can stop the flow of wealth.

- **Gratitude Invites Wealth**: Shifting to a grateful mindset, even for small amounts of money, leads to more financial opportunities.

- **Law of Attraction Applies to Money**: Focusing on abundance and gratitude brings more wealth, while focusing on lack attracts scarcity.

- **Reflecting on Past Money**: Acknowledging how money has supported you in the past helps develop a sense of financial gratitude.

- **Gratitude for Present Money**: Appreciating the money you currently have opens the door for more to come.

- **Gratitude in Tough Times**: Practicing gratitude during financial challenges increases positive energy, attracting more money.

- **Beliefs Shape Financial Reality**: Limiting beliefs like "I can't afford this" hold you back; changing these beliefs can transform your financial life.

- **Positive Affirmations Shift Beliefs**: Repeating affirmations like "I can afford this" helps replace limiting beliefs with abundant thinking.

- **Gratitude and Mindset Attract Abundance**: The combination of gratitude and a positive mindset creates a powerful magnet for financial prosperity.

CHAPTER 6

GRATITUDE AT WORK - A KEY TO SUCCESS AND FULFILLMENT

"Gratitude unlocks the fullness of life. It turns what we have into enough, and more."

- Melody Beattie

Work is a big part of our lives, and how we feel about it can impact how successful and fulfilled we are. Just like in other areas of life, gratitude plays a key role in creating abundance at work. If you're feeling stuck, stressed, or unappreciated in your job, it might help to take a step back and look at the energy you're putting out. Are you focused on what's going wrong or what you're thankful for?

When was the last time you felt grateful for your job or the work you do? Even if you're facing challenges, there's always something to appreciate, and when you focus on those things, your mindset—and your work life—can shift in amazing ways.

One of my clients, Priya, used to feel very stressed at her job. She often felt undervalued and could only see what wasn't working—

the long hours, a demanding boss, and lack of recognition. But when we started working on gratitude, things began to change.

Priya started focusing on the good parts of her job—like the supportive coworkers, the new skills she was learning, and the financial security it gave her. Over time, her work situation improved, and she even got the promotion she had been hoping for.

How Gratitude Can Change Your Work Life

When you bring gratitude into your work life, it can really change the way you see things. Instead of just noticing the problems, you start seeing opportunities for growth. Gratitude helps you feel more positive, even in tough situations.

Another friend of mine, Rahul, had a lot of issues with conflict at work. He felt like his team didn't understand him, and it made him frustrated.

When we talked about practicing gratitude, even during tough times, he decided to give it a try. Rahul started appreciating the feedback he got from his team, even when it was hard to hear. He saw it as a chance to improve. This small shift made a big difference. His relationships with his coworkers improved, and he was soon recognized for his leadership skills.

Being Grateful for Your Current Job

No matter what job you have, there's always something to appreciate. It could be the stability it gives you, the people you work with, or the chance to learn new things. If you're feeling stuck, try to focus on what's going right, even if it's small. Gratitude isn't just for the good days—it's for all days.

For example, instead of thinking, "I'm not where I want to be in my career," try focusing on what your current job offers. Maybe it's helping you develop skills that will lead to your next opportunity. Gratitude helps you shift from a mindset of lack to one of abundance, and that's when you start seeing better results.

Gratitude Attracts Success

People who are grateful at work tend to be more positive, engaged, and resilient, which leads to more success. When you express gratitude to others—whether it's your boss, coworkers, or clients—it builds stronger relationships. Appreciation creates a sense of trust and cooperation, which makes it easier to succeed.

When you feel grateful for your job, no matter how small or big the positives, you also start to feel more confident. And that confidence draws success toward you. You're more open to opportunities and less focused on what's lacking.

Finding Gratitude in Difficult Situations

It's not always easy to feel grateful when things aren't going well at work, but this is when gratitude can help the most. Even during challenging times, you can usually find something to appreciate. Maybe a difficult project is helping you develop resilience, or a demanding boss is teaching you time management. Seeing challenges as opportunities makes it easier to deal with them.

One of my clients, Raj, worked in sales and always felt overwhelmed by the pressure to meet targets. He was frustrated and wanted to quit.

But when he started practicing gratitude—focusing on the skills he was building and the ways he was growing—his outlook changed. Instead of feeling weighed down, he saw the pressure as a chance to improve. Soon, Raj started meeting and even exceeding his sales goals.

Creating a Culture of Gratitude at Work

Gratitude is contagious. When you practice it, others will follow. A workplace filled with gratitude has higher morale, better teamwork, and more productivity.

If you're in a leadership role, showing gratitude toward your team can make a big difference. When employees feel appreciated, they're more engaged and motivated.

But even if you're not a leader, expressing gratitude to your coworkers can help create a more positive work environment for everyone.

Conclusion: Gratitude Leads to Success

Work can be tough, but when you bring gratitude into your daily routine, it can change everything. It shifts your focus from what's not working to what is.

It helps you build stronger relationships, learn from challenges, and attract more success. Gratitude might seem simple, but it's incredibly powerful in transforming how you feel about work and life.

Start practicing gratitude today. Reflect on what you appreciate about your work, even the small things. With time, you'll notice that your work life feels more fulfilling, and you may even find new doors opening up for you.

****

Simple Steps to Practice Gratitude at Work:

1. **Focus on the Positives**:

   o   Each day, think of three things you're grateful for at work, like a helpful coworker or a learning experience.

2. **Thank Your Colleagues**:

   o   Make it a habit to thank the people you work with for their efforts, even for the small things.

3. **See the Good in Challenges**:

   o   When work feels tough, ask yourself, "What am I learning from this?" Try to appreciate the growth that comes with challenges.

4. **Keep a Gratitude Journal**:

   o   At the end of each workday, write down one thing you're grateful for that happened, even on tough days.

5. **Turn Complaints into Gratitude**:

   o   When you catch yourself feeling negative about work, pause and think of something to be grateful for in that moment.

By practicing these simple steps, you'll start to see your work life shift, and you'll feel more fulfilled and successful in what you do.

Key Takeaways:

1. **Gratitude shifts your focus from problems to opportunities**:

   o By practicing gratitude, you start seeing the good in your work situation, which opens up new possibilities.

2. **Gratitude improves your work relationships**:

   o Appreciating coworkers and supervisors helps build stronger, more positive connections, leading to better teamwork and collaboration.

3. **Gratitude boosts your success**:

   o Feeling grateful increases confidence and positivity, making you more open to opportunities and success.

4. **Even tough situations offer something to be grateful for**:

   o Challenges at work can help you grow and develop new skills. Gratitude helps you see difficulties as learning opportunities.

5. **Gratitude is contagious**:

   o When you express gratitude at work, others notice and often follow, creating a more positive and productive environment.

6. **Gratitude leads to fulfillment**:

   o By focusing on what's going well and appreciating your current job, you'll feel more satisfied and content in your career.

7. **A culture of gratitude increases productivity**:

   o Teams that practice gratitude tend to be more engaged, motivated, and productive, resulting in greater success.

These takeaways show that gratitude isn't just about feeling good—it's a powerful tool for creating success, fulfillment, and positive change at work.

CHAPTER 7

INCORPORATING GRATITUDE: SIMPLE STEPS TO MAKE IT A HABIT

Gratitude is the simplest way to change your outlook, improve your life, and attract positivity.

Gratitude is something that can easily become a natural part of your daily life with just a little effort. It's not complicated, and the more you practice, the more you'll start to feel its benefits. I'm going to walk you through some simple steps to help you build gratitude into your life so it becomes a habit you don't even have to think about.

1. Start with Small Moments of Gratitude

You don't have to wait for something huge to happen to feel grateful. It's actually the little things that make the biggest difference. Start by noticing small blessings in your day—like a good cup of coffee, a nice breeze, or just having a comfortable place to sit. Pause for a second, and just say "thank you" in your mind.

For example, my friend Riya used to feel overwhelmed by life. She began focusing on tiny things—her favorite breakfast, a peaceful walk, or a chat with a friend. After a while, she started to feel happier and more at peace.

2. Create a Daily Gratitude Ritual

One of the best ways to make gratitude a habit is to build it into your routine. You can do this by setting aside just a few minutes in the morning or before bed to think of three things you're grateful for. Write them down if you want—it helps to make it stick.

I know Amit, who was really stressed out from his job, started writing down three things he was thankful for every night. At first, it felt strange, but within a week, he started feeling better, and his stress reduced.

3. Gratitude Journaling

If you enjoy writing, keeping a gratitude journal is a great way to go deeper. Every day, jot down a few things you're thankful for. They don't have to be big things—just moments or experiences from the day.

The beauty of a journal is that on days when you're feeling down, you can look back and remind yourself of all the good things you have in life. It's a really simple and effective way to shift your mood.

Whenever I feel stuck or frustrated, I look back at my own gratitude journal, and it helps me regain perspective and feel more grounded.

4. Express Gratitude to Others

Gratitude isn't just something we feel—it's something we can share. One of the best ways to make it a habit is to thank the people around you. It could be a quick "thank you" to a friend, a co-worker, or even someone who helps you with small things, like the barista who makes your coffee.

I remember Amit began thanking his colleagues for their support, even for little things. This simple act of gratitude really improved his relationships at work.

5. Use Gratitude Affirmations

Affirmations are simple statements that help you stay focused on the good. You can start by repeating short, positive phrases to yourself, like, "I am grateful for the abundance in my life," or "I am thankful for the support of my loved ones."

You can say them out loud in the morning, while driving, or whenever you need a little boost. Affirmations help keep your mind focused on the positive.

Personally, I use affirmations every morning. It's a quick and easy way to start the day with a grateful heart.

6. Reflect on Challenges with Gratitude

This one might be harder, but it's also the most rewarding. Even when you're going through tough times, try to find one small thing to be grateful for.

Maybe you're learning something from the situation, or maybe it's showing you how strong you are.

Riya told me that after a tough setback at work, she started looking for the positives, even in that challenge.

It wasn't easy, but over time, it helped her see things in a more positive light.

7. Turn Gratitude into a Fun Challenge

If you're having trouble staying consistent, make gratitude fun. Challenge yourself to find five things you're grateful for each day, or turn it into a game with friends or family. It doesn't have to be serious all the time—gratitude can be playful too.

For instance, Amit turned it into a family game where they each shared things they were grateful for over dinner.

It was a fun way for them to bond and stay positive.

8. Set Gratitude Reminders

We all get busy and forget to practice gratitude sometimes, so setting reminders can be helpful. You can put sticky notes around the house, set an alarm on your phone, or keep a gratitude jar where you drop in little notes every time something good happens.

These small reminders will help you stay on track, even on the busiest days.

Conclusion: Making Gratitude a Part of You

Building gratitude into your life is simple and doesn't take much time. By following these easy steps, you'll find that gratitude becomes second nature. Whether it's writing things down, saying thank you to others, or using affirmations, each small effort adds up. The more you practice, the more you'll feel the benefits, even when life gets challenging.

Key Takeaways:

Start small: Focus on the everyday moments, like enjoying a good meal or feeling a cool breeze.

Daily routine: Take a few minutes each day, either morning or night, to reflect on what you're grateful for.

Gratitude journaling: Write down your thoughts in a journal. It helps to remind you of the good things in your life.

Thank others: Share your gratitude with those around you—it strengthens relationships and spreads positivity.

Affirmations: Use positive gratitude statements to keep yourself focused on the good.

Find gratitude in tough times: Look for small lessons or silver linings, even in difficult situations.

Make it fun: Turn gratitude into a game or challenge to keep it light and engaging.

Use reminders: Sticky notes, phone alarms, or a gratitude jar can help you stay consistent in practicing gratitude.

By following these simple steps, you'll find that gratitude becomes a natural part of your life, bringing more happiness, fulfillment, and success.

CHAPTER 8

THE GRATITUDE DILEMMA: WHY THE FREQUENCY FADES

Gratitude is one of those things that everyone loves in the beginning, but it seems to fade away after a while, right? I've seen this happen with so many of the people I coach. They start strong, feeling thankful every day, but after a few weeks, the enthusiasm fades. So why does this happen? Let me share a few stories to explain.

I once had a client, Priya, who was so excited when she started her gratitude practice. Every night, she'd write down three things she was grateful for. In the first week, she was bursting with energy. She would say, "Sanya, I feel so positive, like everything is going my way!" But by the third or fourth week, she started skipping days. Eventually, she told me she wasn't feeling the same spark anymore.

This happens to many of us. When we first start practicing gratitude, it feels amazing. We notice the small things, feel more connected, and everything seems brighter. But over time, it starts to feel repetitive. The high of those first few weeks fades. You might even catch yourself thinking, *"Do I really have to do this again?"*

So, why does the frequency of gratitude fade?

1. We Get Too Comfortable

When something becomes a routine, we start to take it for granted. Think about it—when you get a new phone or a new car, you're super excited at first. You're grateful for how well it works, or how good it looks. But after a few months? It's just a part of your life, and you stop noticing it.

The same thing happens with gratitude. When you first start, it's fresh and exciting. But as the days go by, you get used to the practice, and it starts to lose that spark.

Another one of my clients, Rahul, experienced this. When he began practicing gratitude, he was grateful for his job, his home, and his family. After a few weeks, though, he started feeling like he was just going through the motions. "I'm still grateful for my job," he said, "but I don't feel the same excitement when I write it down."

2. We Stop Being Specific

Gratitude loses its power when we're not specific enough. If you keep writing "I'm thankful for my family" every day, it can start to feel empty. You need to dig deeper.

Take my friend Anjali, for example. She was practicing gratitude every morning, but eventually, it became a checklist for her. "I'm grateful for my health, my home, my family," she would say without much thought.

But when I asked her to get more specific, things changed. Instead of just being thankful for her family, she started writing things like, "I'm thankful for my daughter's laughter today," or "I'm grateful for the way my husband supported me during a tough conversation." Suddenly, her gratitude practice became meaningful again.

3. We Focus on the Big Things and Forget the Small Moments

It's easy to feel grateful for the obvious blessings in our lives—like a promotion at work or a big family celebration. But the real magic of gratitude lies in noticing the small, everyday moments.

One of my coaching clients, Rakesh, came to me feeling stuck. He was practicing gratitude daily but didn't feel like it was making a difference. When we looked deeper, I realized he was only focusing on the big things, like his job or a recent bonus. I suggested he shift his focus to smaller moments.

The next time we talked, he told me he had written down that he was grateful for the quiet moment he had with his cup of tea in the morning. That small shift changed everything for him.

4. We Start Focusing on What We Don't Have

Gratitude fades when we stop appreciating what we have and start focusing on what's missing. It's easy to get caught up in thinking about the next goal, the next achievement, or the next thing we want.

I had a client, Meera, who told me she had stopped feeling grateful because she was always thinking about what she hadn't achieved yet. She was grateful for her career, but she kept focusing on how much further she wanted to go.

This shifted her energy from gratitude to lack, and it made her feel stuck. When she started focusing again on the things she already had—like the supportive colleagues and the exciting projects at work—her gratitude practice revived.

****

So, how do we keep gratitude alive?

1. Stay Specific

Instead of general statements like "I'm grateful for my job," get specific. What about your job makes you grateful today? Is it the supportive conversation you had with a coworker, or the way a project turned out? The more specific, the better.

2. Look for Small Wins

Don't wait for the big events to feel grateful. Start noticing the little things—like the warmth of the sun, or a kind word from a friend. These small moments add up and keep the gratitude flowing.

3. Be Present

Gratitude fades when we're always looking ahead or behind. Stay present. Appreciate the now, not just what's coming or what's past.

4. Change It Up

Try mixing up your gratitude practice. If you're getting bored, switch from writing it down to saying it out loud, or try sharing it with a friend or family member. Sometimes a simple change in how you practice can reignite the feeling.

5. Take Time to Reflect

Every few weeks, reflect on your gratitude practice. What's working? What isn't? This reflection helps you stay intentional and prevents the practice from becoming stale.

Inculcating Gratitude into Our Daily Lives

The key to keeping gratitude alive is to make it part of your daily routine, so it becomes second nature.

You don't want it to be something you have to sit down and think about every day. Instead, gratitude should flow naturally through your life—something that's present in every breath you take.

Here are some simple ways to bring gratitude into your everyday routine:

1. Gratitude in Small Moments

Gratitude doesn't have to be a formal practice. You can practice it in small moments throughout your day. For example, when you're drinking your morning coffee, take a second to feel grateful for that warm cup in your hands.

When you're walking, be thankful for the ability to move your body. These small moments of appreciation add up.

I suggested this to one of my clients, Asha, who struggled to find time for a formal gratitude practice. Instead of writing in a journal, she started to pause for a moment before meals to be grateful for the food on her plate.

She told me it helped her feel more connected to gratitude in her everyday life.

2. Link Gratitude to Existing Habits

An easy way to make gratitude part of your life is to link it to something you're already doing. For example, you could express gratitude every time you brush your teeth or take a shower. This helps gratitude become automatic, so you don't even have to think about it.

I had a client, Nikhil, who would always forget to write in his gratitude journal. So I suggested that he express gratitude while brushing his teeth. He'd say, "I'm grateful for this moment of peace," or "I'm thankful for my health." Over time, it became such a habit that he didn't even need to remind himself.

3. Gratitude Before Bed

Before you go to sleep at night, think about one thing that happened during the day that you're grateful for. This doesn't have to be something big—it could be as simple as a nice conversation with a friend or a good meal. By ending your day with gratitude, you'll go to bed with a positive mindset.

My friend Riya does this every night. She used to lie awake thinking about all the things she needed to do the next day, but now she ends her day by thinking of something she's thankful for. It helps her sleep better and wakes up feeling more positive.

Key Takeaways:

- Gratitude fades when it becomes routine, but staying specific and focused on small moments can reignite its power.

- Avoid focusing on what's missing and instead appreciate what's present, no matter how small.

- Regular reflection can help you keep your gratitude practice fresh and meaningful.

- Mixing up how you express gratitude—through writing, speaking, or sharing—can help keep the energy alive.

- Small moments of gratitude, when noticed and appreciated, can make a big impact over time.

****

Remember, gratitude is a journey, not a destination. Like any practice, it will have its ups and downs. But when you stay mindful and present, it can transform your life, just like it has for so many of the people I've worked with.

CHAPTER 9

GRATITUDE: THE JOURNEY CONTINUES

As we come to the end of this book, I want to remind you that gratitude is not a destination. It's a journey—one that continues for the rest of your life. This practice of gratitude is like a seed that you've planted, and now, you have the chance to nurture it and watch it grow.

Many people think that once they start practicing gratitude, they'll master it after a while and be done with it. But gratitude is like any other skill; it needs ongoing attention, practice, and nurturing. You don't reach a point where you've "completed" your gratitude practice. Instead, it becomes part of who you are, evolving with you as you grow.

I remember one of my long-time clients, Maya, who came to me years ago feeling lost and disconnected. Gratitude was something she had never really thought about, let alone practiced. But over the years, she made it a part of her life. Even after she experienced some tough moments—like the loss of a job—she continued to lean on her gratitude practice to guide her through. Today, she tells me that gratitude is something she carries with her in every moment, not just during the good times.

Gratitude in the Ups and Downs

Life will always have its ups and downs. Gratitude is not about pretending that everything is perfect. It's about finding something to appreciate even when things are hard. One of the most beautiful things about gratitude is that it teaches us to see the good in every situation, even when we're struggling.

I had a friend, Arjun, who went through a rough patch when his business was failing. It was hard for him to see anything positive. But instead of focusing only on what wasn't working, he began to focus on what he still had—his supportive family, his health, and the lessons he was learning through his challenges. Over time, his business turned around, but it was his gratitude that helped him stay grounded and positive during those tough times.

The journey of gratitude continues because life continues. Every new day brings new opportunities to practice gratitude. Sometimes, it will be easy—you'll feel naturally thankful for something amazing that's happened. Other times, it will be harder, and you'll have to dig a little deeper to find something to appreciate. But the more you practice, the easier it becomes to find those moments of gratitude, no matter what's going on in your life.

Gratitude Beyond the Obvious

As you move forward, I encourage you to go beyond the obvious when it comes to gratitude. Of course, it's easy to be thankful for the big things like a new job, a loving relationship, or a beautiful home. But true gratitude is about seeing the blessings in the small, everyday moments.

One of my clients, Seema, shared with me how she started feeling grateful for things she used to overlook—like the way the sunlight streamed through her window in the morning or the sound of her favorite song playing in the background while she worked. These small moments might seem insignificant, but when you start noticing them, your whole perspective changes. Life becomes richer and more fulfilling.

Gratitude can be found in the simplest things: a kind smile from a stranger, the warmth of a cozy blanket on a cold night, or the feeling of peace after a long day.

When you start to notice and appreciate these little things, you realize that there's so much to be grateful for, even in the most ordinary days.

Let Gratitude Become Who You Are

The goal is to let gratitude become part of who you are, not just something you "do." When gratitude becomes a way of being, it's with you in every breath, every thought, and every action. You won't have to remind yourself to practice gratitude—it will naturally flow through you.

One of my clients, Kiran, used to struggle with making gratitude a habit. She had to constantly remind herself to write in her journal or pause to give thanks. But over time, she noticed that gratitude started to show up in her life without effort. She'd catch herself feeling grateful in the middle of the day, for no specific reason, just because she was so tuned into the abundance around her.

This is what the journey of gratitude is all about. It's about reaching a point where you don't have to sit down and think, *"What am I grateful for today?"* Instead, you just feel it, naturally and effortlessly. It's in your breath, in your thoughts, in your daily routine. It becomes part of your essence.

The Ripple Effect of Gratitude

What's amazing about gratitude is that it doesn't just impact you—it affects everyone around you. When you live with gratitude, you start to spread that energy to others. Your positive outlook, your appreciation for life, and your ability to see the good in any situation inspire the people around you.

I've seen this ripple effect happen with one of my clients, Ravi. He started practicing gratitude to improve his own mindset, but over time, he noticed that it was affecting his family too. His children started practicing gratitude, and even his wife, who used to be skeptical about it, began to appreciate the small things more. It created a more positive and peaceful atmosphere in their home.

Gratitude is contagious. When you live in a state of gratitude, others can feel it. You become a source of positivity and inspiration for the people around you, whether it's your family, friends, or even coworkers.

The Journey Continues

As you move forward in life, remember that the journey of gratitude never ends. There will always be new opportunities to practice it, new lessons to learn, and new moments to appreciate. Life will continue to surprise you with its beauty and challenges, and through it all, gratitude will be your guide.

When you choose to live with gratitude, you open yourself up to more abundance, more joy, and more peace. It's not always an easy path, but it's one that will continue to enrich your life in ways you can't even imagine.

So, as you close this book, take a moment to reflect on the journey you've begun. Remember that gratitude is always there for you, waiting to be embraced. Keep walking this path, and watch as your life continues to bloom with the power of gratitude.

****

Key Takeaways:

- Gratitude is a lifelong journey, not a destination. It requires ongoing practice and nurturing.

- Life will have ups and downs, but gratitude helps you stay grounded and find the good, even in tough times.

- Go beyond the obvious—notice and appreciate the small, everyday moments.

- Let gratitude become part of who you are, not just something you do. It should flow naturally through your life.

- Gratitude has a ripple effect, positively impacting the people around you and creating a more positive environment.

- The journey of gratitude continues throughout your life, offering more opportunities for joy, peace, and abundance.

****

Gratitude isn't something you check off your list; it's something that grows with you. As you continue this journey, know that gratitude will always be there to support you, guiding you toward a richer, more fulfilling life.

Disclaimer

This book is intended for informational and inspirational purposes only. The content within is based on personal experiences, research, and insights into the practice of gratitude. It is not a substitute for professional medical, psychological, financial, or legal advice. Readers are encouraged to use their discretion and seek professional guidance when necessary. The author and publisher assume no responsibility for any outcomes resulting from the application of the concepts discussed in this book.

By reading this book, you acknowledge that the practice of gratitude is a personal journey, and results may vary for each individual.

About the Author

Sanya Kapoor is a life coach, healer, and law of attraction expert dedicated to helping people cultivate happiness, success, and abundance. Through her work in coaching, conflict training, and mindset transformation, she has guided countless individuals toward achieving their goals with gratitude and positivity.

Her passion for personal growth and manifestation inspired her to write this book, where she shares insights on gratitude, money beliefs, and how shifting one's mindset can attract abundance. Sanya believes that small changes in perspective can lead to powerful transformations, and she is committed to making these teachings accessible to everyone.

In addition to her book, Sanya shares her wisdom through her YouTube channel, coaching programs, and online workshops, helping people create a fulfilling life.

When she's not coaching or writing, Sanya enjoys spending time with Sajal, exploring new ideas, and practicing the principles she teaches.

Connect with Sanya on YouTube: @casanyakapoor

May I Ask You For A Small Favor?

First, I want to thank you for reading this book. You could have chosen any other book, but you took mine, and I appreciate this. I hope you have at least a few actionable insights that will positively impact your daily life.

Can I ask for 30 seconds more of your time?

I'd love it if you could leave a review of the book. That will help me grow my readership by encouraging folks to take a chance on my books.

Keeping it straight - reviews are the lifeblood of any author.

It will take less than a minute of your time but will tremendously help me reach out to more people.

If you liked this book, please consider posting an honest review on your preferred retailer. And I'd love to see your review. Thanks for your support.